D1520165

To Arlo

BECAUSE YOU'RE YOU...

A Very Special Guy

"

Love
Mom

The C. R. Gibson Company
Norwalk, Connecticut

Here's to you!
Enjoy!

SUNSHINE

When a man feels weary or depressed or in pain, just stepping into clear sunshine does something to him. I have felt it often. Sunshine is manifestly more than heat and light and invisible rays—even as the whole can be greater than the sum of its parts. It is something subtler, nearer to the spiritual, something close to the quick of life itself. It seems to me that the sun has in some degree the quality of a patriarchal blessing—a bestowal of that special feeling of security that comes through the love of dear parents still living in the old family homestead where one was born and raised.

For the sun is truly the birthstead of the whole earth.

GUY MURCHIE

BY DAWN'S EARLY LIGHT

Unless a man is up for the dawn and for the half-hour or so of first light, he has missed the best of the day. The traffic has just started. One car at a time goes by, the tires humming almost like the sound of a brook a half-mile down in the crease of a mountain I know—a sound that carries not because it is loud but because everything else is still.

It isn't exactly a mist that hangs in the thickets, but more nearly the ghost of a mist—it will be gone three minutes after the sun comes over the treetops. The lawns shine with a dew not exactly dew. There is a rabbit bobbing about on the lawn and then freezing. If it were truly a dew, his tracks would shine black on the grass, and he leaves no visible track. Yet, there is something on the grass that makes it glow a depth of green it will not show again all day. Or is that something in the dawn air?

There is a mountain laurel on the island of the driveway turnaround. From somewhere on the wind, a white morning glory rooted near it and climbed it. The laurel is woven full of white bells tinged pink by the first rays through the not-quite mist. Only in earliest morning can the morning glories be seen.

And now the sun is slanting in full. The leaves of the Japanese red maple seem a transparent red-bronze when the tree is between me and the light. This is the only tree I know whose leaves let the sun through in this way—except, that is, when the fall colors start. Green takes sunlight and holds it; red and yellow let it through.

I hear a brake-squeak and know that the newspaper has arrived. As usual, the news turns out to be another disaster count. I sit on the patio and read until the sun grows too bright on the page. The cardinals have stopped singing, and the grackles have flown off.

Then suddenly—better, for its instant, than song—a hummingbird the color of green crushed-velvet hovers in the throat of my favorite lily, a lovely high-bloomer. The lily is a crest of white horns with red dots and red-velvet tongues along the insides of the petals and with an odor that drowns the patio. The hummingbird darts in and out of each horn, then hovers an instant and disappears.

Even without the sun's glare, I have had enough of the paper. I'll take that hummingbird as my news for this dawn. It is over now.

JOHN CIARDI

MAN CANNOT MAKE WILDNESS

It is fair to remember that
     this is not a land that belongs to us.
     We cannot destroy it without destroying
          something in us.
Its trees can teach us tenacity
     and patience and serenity and respect.
Life's urge to survive is the force
     that shaped them and their world of wildness,
     that made them one of the great miracles.
Man, if he is too impatient to care,
     can end this miracle, can terminate a
          chain of life
     going back without interruption to an
          old eternity,
or man, able to create ideas, can meet his
     old material needs with a different urge—
     an urge to preserve what he cannot replace.

Wildness made man but man cannot make wildness.
     He can only spare it.

                                        DAVID BROWER

SKATING FREE

I wonder how many of the 400,000 kids on 20,000 teams across Canada ever played a hockey game without shin pads, hockey pants, elbow pads, shoulder pads and gloves; without a referee and a time clock, without a coach and a dressing room. I am not going to claim it was much better when we had old magazines stuffed down our pants, and used frozen apples for pucks, or that it was nice to change into our skates outdoors. In many ways I envy my two sons their numbered sweaters and their goals-and-assists records. But there is one day I'll bet they'd envy me.

A bunch of us, 10 or 11 years old, were playing our usual six-hour Saturday game, outdoors, in a boarded-off part of the ball park. Someone shot the puck over the boards and someone else went after it. Amazingly, he found that his skates didn't break the snow. It had rained the night before, and the sharp cold had hardened the rain into a solid crust; instead of walking to the puck, he was able to glide. Tentatively, he shot the puck farther across the park. It slid for at least a rink length, and he called to us. One by one we raced across the frozen snow after him, laughing and yelling as we found that we could skate across the open.

Away we went, across the fairgrounds and the football field, then up a hill and down, our skates still not cutting the snow. And out of the park we went, across city streets and down lanes and out into the country—as untrammelled as birds in the clean crisp air, winging our way across hills and around trees.

We skated miles that day, going anywhere we wanted to, sometimes leaving the puck behind, sometimes playing hockey with half a mile between the goals—the whole world an outdoor rink.

I wish all boys on skates could have that experience at least once.

PETER GZOWSKI

To speak truly, few adults can see nature . . . The sun illuminates only the eye of the man, but shines into the eye and the heart of the child. The lover of nature is he whose inward and outward senses are still truly adjusted to each other, who has retained the spirit of infancy even into the era of manhood.

RALPH WALDO EMERSON

A LARGE PART OF FOREVER

June meant, when I was a small boy in a small Nebraska town, that school was out and we had a whole summer ahead. Summer was endless. It was June, July and August, and three whole months in a small boy's life was a large part of forever.

I am quite sure, looking back, that we kids were the originators of the do-it-yourself movement, and I feel that today's youngsters are woefully deprived. Every time I go to the village I see youngsters buying things to have fun with. Maybe it's just a part of this vicarious way of life we have evolved, but I say the kids miss half the fun. I doubt that any of us kids had more than a dollar to spend all summer, and we spent most of that for fireworks for the Fourth of July. But we all had jackknives and ingenuity, and what an ingenious boy can do with a jackknife is worth watching. Or remembering.

HAL BORLAND

We listen too much to the telephone and we listen too little to nature. The wind is one of my sounds. A lonely sound, perhaps, but soothing. Everybody should have his personal sounds to listen for—sounds that will make him exhilarated and alive, or quiet and calm. . . . As a matter of fact, one of the greatest sounds of them all—and to me it is a sound—is utter complete silence.

ANDRÉ KOSTELANETZ

The oldest voice in the world is the wind. When it murmurs in summer's leaves, it seems an idle trifler. When in the night it goes wandering by, setting the old house faintly to groaning, it sounds like a pilgrim that has lost the road. When you see it fitfully turning the blades of a mill lazily to draw water, you think of it as an unreliable servant of man. But in truth it is one of our masters, obedient only to the lord sun and the whirling of the great globe itself.

DONALD CULROSS PEATTIE

THE SOUND OF TREES

I wonder about the trees.
Why do we wish to bear
Forever the noise of these
More than another noise
So close to our dwelling place?
We suffer them by the day
Till we lose all measure of pace,
And fixity in our joys,
And acquire a listening air.
They are that that talks of going
But never gets away;
And that talks no less for knowing,
As it grows wiser and older,
That now it means to stay.
My feet tug at the floor
And my head sways to my shoulder
Sometimes when I watch trees sway,
From the window or the door.
I shall set forth for somewhere,
I shall make the reckless choice
Some day when they are in voice
And tossing so as to scare
The white clouds over them on.
I shall have less to say,
But I shall be gone.

ROBERT FROST

TO JAMES

Do you remember
How you won
That last race . . . ?
How you flung your body
At the start . . .
How your spikes
Ripped the cinders
In the stretch . . .
How you catapulted
Through the tape . . .
Do you remember . . . ?
Don't you think
I lurched with you
Out of those starting holes . . . ?
Don't you think
My sinews tightened
At those first
Few strides . . .
And when you flew into the stretch
Was not all my thrill
Of a thousand races
In your blood . . . ?
At your final drive
Through the finish line
Did not my shout
Tell of the
Triumphant ecstasy
Of victory . . . ?

Live
As I have taught you
To run, Boy—
It's a short dash
Dig your starting holes
Deep and firm
Lurch out of them
Into the straightaway
With all the power
That is in you
Look straight ahead
To the finish line
Think only of the goal
 Run straight
 Run high
 Run hard
 Save nothing
 And finish
 With an ecstatic burst
 That carries you
 Hurtling
 Through the tape
 To victory. . . .

                    FRANK HORNE

SPORTS

The pleasure of sport was so often the chance to indulge the cessation of time itself—the pitcher dawdling on the mound, the skier poised at the top of a mountain trail, the basketball player with the rough skin of the ball against his palm preparing for a foul shot, the tennis player at set point over his opponent—all of them savoring a moment before committing themselves to action.

GEORGE PLIMPTON

SPORTS—PRO AND CON

Golf is an awkward set of bodily contortions designed to produce a graceful result.

TOMMY ARMOUR

This would be a fine world if all men showed as much patience all the time as they do when they're waiting for a fish to bite.

THE HUB, Tampa, Fla.

The nature of tennis and its demands usually make a good player out of a fellow who has trouble playing any other game, including tiddlywinks.

BOB CONSIDINE

Golf is like a love affair: if you don't take it seriously, it's no fun; if you do take it seriously, it breaks your heart.

ARNOLD DALY

Here is no sentiment, no contest, no grandeur, no economics. From the sanctity of this occupation, a man may emerge refreshed and in control of his own soul. He is not idle. He is fishing, alone with himself in dignity and peace. It seems a very precious thing to me.

JOHN STEINBECK

Of all the competitive sports, a strong case can be made for skiing as the most emotional, the most exciting, the most satisfying. It may be the most difficult of all sports. Victory, then, is so much sweeter.

MAURY ALLEN

DUEL WITH A DEVIL

A strange calm settled over me as I stood before the large white vending machine and dropped in a quarter. When the coin clunked, I pressed the button marked "Hot Chocolate." A paper cup slid down a chute, crackling into place on a small metal rack. Through an unseen tube poured coffee, black as night.

I even smiled as I moved to my customary place at the last table in the snack bar, sat down and gazed across to the white machine, large and clean and defiant. Every morning for two weeks I had selected a beverage, and each time the machine had dispensed something different. So the coffee before me was no surprise. It was but one final test; my plan had already been laid.

After everyone else had left the building, I returned to the snack bar, a yellow pad in my hand and a fistful of change in my pocket. I approached the machine and began feeding in quarters. After the first quarter, I pressed the "Black Coffee" button. Tea with sugar came out, and I recorded that on my pad. I dropped in a second quarter, and chose coffee with sugar. Plain tea came out, and I wrote that down.

I pressed all nine buttons, noting what came out. Then I placed each cup on the table behind me. I now repeated the selection process, and was delighted to find that each error was consistent with my list.

To celebrate, I decided to purchase a fresh cup of hot chocolate. Dropping in two dimes and a nickel, and consulting my pad, I pressed "Coffee with Sugar and Half-and-Half." The machine clicked in response, and a little cup slid down the chute. But no hot chocolate poured into my cup. No black coffee. Nothing.

I was livid. I put in five more nickels and pushed another button. Another cup dropped down—empty. I dug into my pocket, found three dimes and forced them in. I got back a stream of hot water and a nickel change. I went berserk.

"White devil!" I screamed as I slammed my fists against the machine's clean enamel finish. I beat on the buttons and rammed the coin-return rod. I kicked the base with such force that I could almost hear the bone in my foot crack, then wheeled in agony on my good foot and with one frantic swing sent the entire tableful of cups sailing.

That was last night. They have cleaned up the snack bar since then, and I've had my foot X-rayed and wrapped in that brown elastic they use for sprains. I am now sitting with my back to the row of vending machines. I know by the steadiness of my hand as I pour homemade hot chocolate from my thermos that no one can sense what I have been through—except, of course, the great white machine.

Even now, behind me, in the space just below the coin slot, a tiny sign blinks on and off: "Make Another Selection," it taunts. "Make Another Selection."

SKIP ROZIN

HOW TO KNOW WHETHER TO GET UP AND FIX THE WAY THE TELEVISION PICTURE IS REVOLVING OR WAIT AND SEE IF IT FIXES ITSELF.

This is a serious problem, for the essence of television watching is being able to sit there inertly, and having to get up to fix the picture when it starts revolving spoils the whole thing. Also, if you fix the picture, it may start revolving worse, faster, the other way. What makes matters so perplexing is that if you wait, the TV keeps on doing it; while if you get up, it stops just as you walk toward it. The particular anguish is that there's no way of knowing if the revolving would have stopped if you hadn't got up.

I firmly believe that it wouldn't have stopped. It's not the perversity of "things," but just that it really does help the TV when you walk toward it. I believe that your body being near the thing acts as some kind of extra antenna, in a technical way; and that's what makes it stop revolving when you get up.

Reasoning, then, would lead to the conclusion that you must get up and not wait to see if it fixes itself. But before you get up, for heaven's sake notice which way it is revolving, so that when it stops revolving as you approach it, you can remember which way the adjustment has to be made. Bend your knees quickly, pretending to sit down, then snap straight up again.

Finally, you can try pretending to get up, but I don't think that works, because the TV has a very big eye and sees right into your mind. The best thing to do, ultimately, is just to shut your eyes and listen, peeking every once in a while to see if it has fixed itself.

L. RUST HILLS

I don't know why it is
that we are in such
a hurry to get up
when we fall down.
You might think
we would lie there:
and rest awhile.
                MAX EASTMAN

One of the best ways of avoiding necessary and even urgent
tasks is to seem to be busily employed on things that are
already done.

                                        J. K. GALBRAITH

WORK—A GOOD PART OF LIFE

A man's work is one of the more important parts of his social identity, of his self, indeed of the fate in the one life he has to live, for there is something almost irrevocable about the choice of occupation as there is about the choice of a mate.

EVERETT HUGHES

Efficiency of a practically
flawless kind may be reached
naturally in the struggle for
bread. But there is something
beyond—a higher point, a
subtle and unmistakable touch
of love and pride beyond mere
skill; almost an inspiration
which gives to all work that
finish what is almost
art—which is art.

JOSEPH CONRAD

The world is full of willing people; some willing to work, the rest willing to let them.

ROBERT FROST

I've met a few people in my time who were enthusiastic about hard work. And it was just my luck that all of them happened to be men I was working for at the time.

BILL GOLD

I like work; it fascinates me. I can sit and look at it for hours.

JEROME K. JEROME

I'm a self-made man, but I think if I had it to do over again, I'd call in someone else.

ROLAND YOUNG

Nobody is sicker than the man who is sick on his day off.

BILL VAUGHAN

FORMER JOBS OF FAMOUS PEOPLE

Desi Arnaz,bandleader	Bird-cage cleaner
Carol Burnett,comedienne	Usherette
James Cagney,actor	Waiter
Johnny Carson,TV personality	Magician
Perry Como,singer	Barber
Howard Cosell,sports announcer	Lawyer
William Faulkner,author	House painter
W. C. Fields,comedian	Juggler
Gerald R. Ford,president	Male model
Clark Gable,actor	Lumberjack
Adolf Hitler,dictator	Poster artist
Bob Hope,comedian	Boxer
Boris Karloff,actor	Real estate salesman
Dean Martin,entertainer	Steelworker
Golda Meir,prime minister	Schoolteacher
Marilyn Monroe,actress	Factory worker
O. Henry,author	Cowboy
Thomas Paine,political author	Corsetmaker
Elvis Presley,singer	Truck driver
Babe Ruth,baseball player	Bartender
Harry S. Truman,president	Haberdasher

WE'LL ALL FEEL BETTER BY WEDNESDAY

I love coffee, I love tea,
I love the girls, but they're mean to me.
I love Saturday, I love Sunday,
But how could anyone ever love Monday?
Let's make a scientific analysis,
Let's diagnose this Monday paralysis.
Well, you've suffered an overdose of sunburn;
You must blister and peel before you un-burn.
For junk your muscles could all be sold for,
From engaging in games you are now too old for.
You're bloated from a diet of buns and hamburgers,
Chickenburgers, cheeseburgers, nutburgers, clamburgers.
Your hair may be brushed, but your mind's untidy,
You've had about seven hours' sleep since Friday,
No wonder you feel that lost sensation;
You're sunk from a riot of relaxation.
What you do on week ends, you claim to adore it.
But Monday's the day that you suffer for it.
That's why Labor Day is a red-letter news day—
Blue Monday doesn't come until Tuesday.

OGDEN NASH

STAR TREKKING

I am sitting here 93 million miles from the sun on a rounded
rock which is spinning at the rate of 1,000 miles per hour,
        and roaring through space to nobody-knows-where, to
keep a rendezvous with nobody-knows-what, for
nobody-knows-why,
        and all around me whole continents are drifting rootlessly
over the surface of the planet,
        India ramming into the underbelly of Asia, part of
America skidding off toward China by way of Alaska,
        Antarctica slipping away from Africa at the rate of an
inch per eon,
        and my head pointing down into space with nothing
between me and infinity but something called gravity which I

can't even understand, and which you can't even buy any
place so as to have some stored away for a gravityless day,
       while off to the north of me the polar icecap may,
       or may not,
       be getting ready to send down oceanic mountains of ice
that will bury everything from Bangor to Richmond,
       and there, off to the east, the ocean is tearing away at the
land and wrenching it into the sea bottom and coming back
for more, as if
       the ocean is determined to claim it all before the deadly
swarms of killer bees,
       which are moving relentlessly northward, from South
America,
       can get there to take possession,
       although it seems more likely that the protective ozone
layer in the upper atmosphere may collapse first,
       exposing us all, ocean, killer bees and me, too,
       to the merciless spraying of deadly cosmic rays.
       I am sitting here on this spinning, speeding rock
surrounded by four billion people,
       eight planets,
       one awesome lot of galaxies,
       hydrogen bombs enough to kill me 30 times over,
       and I am being swept along in the whole galaxy's insane
dash toward the far wall of the universe,
       across distances longer to traverse than Sunday
afternoon on the New Jersey Turnpike,
       so long, in fact, that when we get there I shall be at least
800,000 years old,
       provided, of course, that the whole galaxy doesn't run
into another speeding galaxy at some poorly marked universal

intersection and turn us all into space garbage,
   or that the sun doesn't burn out in the meantime,
   or that some highly intelligent ferns from deepest space
do not land from flying fern pots and cage me up in a
greenhouse for scientific study.
   So, as I say, I am sitting here with the continents moving,
and killer bees coming, and the ocean eating away, and the
galaxy racing across the universe,
   and the thermonuclear 30 times over bombs stacked up
around me,
   and only the gravity holding me onto the rock, which, if
you saw it from Arcturus, you wouldn't be able to see, since it
is so minute that even from these relatively close stars it
would look no bigger than an ant in the Sahara as viewed
from the top of the Empire State Building,
   and as I sit here,
   93 million miles from the sun
   I am feeling absolutely miserable,
   and realize
   with self-pity and despair,
   that I am
   getting a cold.

RUSSELL BAKER

CONFESSIONS OF A BLADE WIPER

No one can say I don't try to cooperate.

In hallways, I walk, don't run. On the subway, I don't smoke, carry lighted matches, spit, or ride between cars. To make sure I keep my hands off the door, I keep them in my pockets. Never in my life have I created a nuisance or an insanitary condition.

I cross at the green, not in between. I don't drive, much less park. I neither litter nor loiter. I post no bills, and I don't play handball where I'm not wanted. I keep off all grass, so naturally I don't pick flowers or start forest fires. I don't try to gain admittance where there is none. I keep out, stand clear.

I don't fold, mutilate, or spindle machine-processed checks. In fact, I smashed my spindle long ago. When I use paper towels I rub, don't blot. This took lots of practice, because I'm a natural-born blotter.

It was only when They started throwing prohibitions at me in my own bathroom that I grew restive. I didn't mind keeping my shaving cream from freezing, but every so often, when I had an empty can, I got this terrible urge to puncture or incinerate it. Recently, I stood in front of the incinerator for fully ten minutes with an empty shaving cream can in one hand and an ice pick in the other, staring at the injunctions on the can and over the incinerator. My conscience won. I incinerated the ice pick and carried the can back to the bathroom, where I stacked it in the tub, together with the twenty-four other empties I don't know how to get rid of. I've been able to take only showers for the last year.

This morning I disobeyed Them at last. I was all excited about trying out these new stainless steel razor blades. I didn't get a bad shave either, so I was feeling pretty good, sort of

romping around, playfully clutching at shaving cream nozzles with my toes, when I saw the words on the box:
NOTICE: DO NOT WIPE BLADE.

That did it! I've been wiping my blades since I shaved the first hairs over my lip. I helped my father wipe his blades before that. I'd rather go to jail than keep a wet blade in any razor of mine overnight. I gave it a good, vigorous wipe. I felt a lifetime of repressions slip instantly from me. I stood straight and tall for the first time in years.

My thumb is still bleeding, but I don't give a rap.

LOU D'ANGELO

LEISURE TIME—TO LOAF OR NOT TO LOAF

Today my heart beat 103,389 times,
my blood traveled 168,000,000 miles,
I breathed 23,040 times,
I inhaled 438 cubic feet of air,
I spoke 4,800 words,
moved 750 major muscles,
and I exercised 7,000,000 brain cells.
I'm tired.

                              BOB HOPE

I have never taken any exercise,
except sleeping and resting,
and I never intend to take any.
Exercise is loathsome.
And it cannot be any benefit
when you are tired;
and I was always tired.

                         MARK TWAIN

Too many people who try to use the weekend to unwind
simply unravel.

BILL COPELAND

When I feel like exercising,
I just lie down
until the feeling goes away.

PAUL TERRY

Don't put off for tomorrow what you can do today, because if
you enjoy it today you can do it again tomorrow.

JAMES A. MICHENER

Living in the lap of luxury isn't so bad except that you never know when luxury is going to stand up.

KEN MURRAY

The original mistake was inventing the calendar. This led, in due course, to having Mondays.

H. V. WADE

The art of fishing brings
meekness and inspiration from
the decency of nature, charity
toward tackle makers, patience
toward fish, a quieting of hate,
and a mockery of profits and
egos. Fishing is great
discipline in the equality of
men—because all men are
equal before fish!

HERBERT HOOVER

If you observe a really happy
man you will find him building
a boat, writing a symphony,
educating his son, growing
double dahlias in his garden,
or looking for dinosaur eggs in
the Gobi desert. He will not be
striving for it as a goal itself.
He will have become aware
that he is happy in the course
of living life twenty-four
crowded hours of the day.

W. BERAN WOLFE

There is one piece of advice, in a life of study, which I
think no one will object to; and that is, every now and then
to be completely idle,—to do nothing at all.

SYDNEY SMITH

THE BACK-YARD CHEF

Most men go through it. It is called the Back Yard Bicarbonate Syndrome, better known to most Americans as the "cookout."

The condition is usually brought about by the acquisition of a new grill, a fun apron that reads, BURNED IS BEAUTIFUL or a neighbor who delights and amazes his guests every weekend with dishes from his new Neanderthal Cookbook.

Somehow you cannot help but admire the courage of these virgin cooks who heretofore thought a pinch of rosemary was something you did when your wife wasn't looking and who considered aspic a ski resort in Colorado.

The big question is how to survive it.

When you are invited to a cookout be sure to check the invitation. If it reads "7 P.M." assume that is the time of arrival. The time you are served may vary as much as forty-eight to seventy-two hours from then depending on:

(a) a confused host who puts the potatoes in the oven and turns on the clothes dryer for 60 minutes;

(b) an emergency visit from the local fire department that got a call that a tire factory is burning;

(c) a group of guests who are all members of the U.S. Olympic Drinking Team and are celebrating their victory over the Russians.

The other night I tripped over my husband who was hunched over his hibachi. "Is that you?" I whispered in the darkness.

"Who did you think it was?" he asked.

"I didn't care. If you hadn't moved I was going to eat you."

"Just a little longer," he said. "Are the guests getting hungry?"

"I think so. They are sitting around watching their stomachs bloat."

"It hasn't been that long."

"Are you kidding? It's the first time I've ever seen my fingernails grow."

"Just a few minutes and the coals will be ready."

"Do you mean to say you haven't even put the meat on yet?"

"Give them some more hors d'oeuvres."

"It's no use. They're beginning to get ugly."

"Then go check everyone and find out how many want their steaks—rare, medium rare, medium, medium well, and well done."

I left and returned in a few minutes.

"Well?" he asked.

"Thirteen raws. Hold the horns."

"Very funny," he said. "How about the fourteenth guest?"

"He ate his coaster and said that would hold him."

"That tears it," he said. "That's the last time I waste my special barbecue sauce on this group of ingrates."

ERMA BOMBECK

How has men's concept of masculinity changed? A poll conducted for Redbook magazine provides a fascinating answer.

Not long ago most American men still thought a man should be brave, stoical, righteous and domineering—a John Wayne figure with a dash of Jehovah thrown in. But as we have seen, things have changed. Most men no longer feel that a man must be the undisputed ruler of the family, the sole breadwinner and the uncontested maker of all important decisions. A good minority of them feel it is not unmanly to work for a female boss, and nearly half say they feel freer today to express deep emotion than they used to.

But the change in men's concept of masculinity goes further. A stock figure of fun (and scorn) in cartoons and movies used to be a man in an apron, washing dishes or running a vacuum cleaner. Today, not only are most husbands willing to share the housework if their wives work, but also 4 out of 5 in every age group deny that they would be embarrassed if others knew they did so. And an overwhelming majority of men say that doing household work does not make them feel less masculine.

MORTON HUNT

Manliness is not all swagger and swearing and mountain climbing. Manliness is also tenderness, gentleness, consideration.

ROBERT ANDERSON

NOTHING CAN VEX LIKE THE OPPOSITE SEX

The best way to hold a man is in your arms.

MAE WEST

A reporter asked Winston
Churchill: "Do you agree with
the prediction that women will
be ruling the world by the year
2000?"
    "Yes," said Churchill,
"they will still be at it."

My advice to the Women's
Clubs of America is to raise
more hell and fewer dahlias.

WILLIAM ALLEN WHITE

I want to make a policy
statement. I am unabashedly
in favor of women.

LYNDON B. JOHNSON

There's nothing like mixing
with women to bring out all the
foolishness in a man of sense.

THORTON WILDER

The allurement that women hold out to men is precisely the
allurement that Cape Hatteras holds out to sailors: they are
enormously dangerous and hence enormously fascinating.

H. L. MENCKEN

Although the opposite sex may occasionally vex, where would one be without the other? Mark Twain comments:

Human intelligence cannot estimate what we owe to woman, sir. She sews on our buttons; she mends our clothes; she ropes us in at the church fairs; she confides in us; she tells us whatever she can find out about the little private affairs of the neighbors; she gives us good advice, and plenty of it; she soothes our aching brows; she bears our children—ours as a general thing.

I repeat, sir, that in whatever position you place a woman she is an ornament to society and a treasure to the world. As a sweetheart she has few equals and no superiors; as a cousin, she is convenient; as a wealthy grandmother with an incurable distemper, she is precious; as a wet nurse, she has no equal among men. What, sir, would the people of the earth be without woman? They would be scarce, sir, almighty scarce.

MARK TWAIN

Acknowledgments

The editor and the publisher have made every effort to trace the ownership of all copyrighted materials and to secure permission from copyright holders of such material. In the event of any question arising as to the use of any material the publisher and editor, while expressing regret for inadvertent error, will be pleased to make the necessary corrections in future printings. Thanks are due to the following authors, publishers, publications and agents for permission to use the material indicated.

CURTIS BROWN,LTD., for excerpt from HILL COUNTRY HARVEST by Hal Borland, copyright © 1967 by Hal Borland.

JAMES BROWN ASSOCIATES, INC., for "Big White" by Skip Rozin, copyright © 1975 by Skip Rozin.

JOHN CIARDI, for excerpt from "Dawn's Early Light," which appeared in the November 6, 1971, issue of Saturday Review, reprinted by permission of the author.

DOUBLEDAY & COMPANY, INC., for excerpt from HOW TO DO THINGS RIGHT, by L. Rust Hills, copyright © 1972 by L. Rust Hills; for excerpt from I LOST EVERYTHING IN THE POST-NATAL DEPRESSION by Erma Bombeck, copyright © 1970, 1971, 1972, 1973 by Field Enterprises, Inc; copyright © 1970, 1971, 1972 by The Hearst Corporation.

HOLT, RINEHART AND WINSTON, for "The Sound of Trees" from THE POETRY OF ROBERT FROST, edited by Edward Connery Lathem, copyright 1916, ©1969 by Holt, Rinehart and Winston, copyright 1944 by Robert Frost.

HOUGHTON MIFFLIN COMPANY, for excerpt from A CUP OF SKY by Donald Culross Peattie; excerpt from MUSIC OF THE SPHERES by Guy Murchie.

HURTIG PUBLISHERS, for excerpt from PETER GZOWSKI'S BOOK ABOUT THIS COUNTRY IN THE MORNING.

ROBERT LESCHER LITERARY AGENCY, for excerpt from "How Has Men's Concept of Masculinity Changed?" by Morton Hunt, copyright © 1976 by Morton Hunt.

MARTIN LEVIN, for "Confessions of a Blade Wiper" by Lou D'Angelo from Martin Levin's PHOENIX NEST, Saturday Review

LITTLE, BROWN AND COMPANY, for "We'll all Feel Better by Wednesday" from VERSUS Ogden Nash, copyright 1949 by Ogden Nash.

WILLIAM MORROW & CO. INC., for "Former Jobs of Famous People" from THE BOOK OF LISTS, copyright 1977.

THE NEW YORK TIMES, for "Star Trekking" by Russell Baker, from the May 18, 1975, issue.

SATURDAY REVIEW, for "Confessions of a Blade Wiper" by Lou D'Angelo from SATURDAY REVIEW SAMPLER OF WIT AND WISDOM, copyright © 1940, 1954, 1955, 1957, 1958, 1960, 1961, 1962, 1963, 1964, 1966 by The Saturday Review.

SIERRA CLUB, for "Man Cannot Make Wilderness" by David Brower, from the Sierra Club Book THE LAST REDWOODS, text by Francois Leydet, photographs by James Rose and others, copyright © 1969 by the Sierra Club.

Designed by Thomas James Aaron

Selected by Eric Robertson

Type set in Korinna Roman

PHOTO CREDITS

Jeffrey Munk—Cover, p.39; Jay Johnson—p.2, p.30, p.47; Maria Demarest—p.6; Elizabeth P. Welsh—p.10; Pat Powers—p.15; State of Vermont—p.19; Bruce Ando—p.23; Four By Five, Inc.—p.35, p.42; Klauss Brahmst—p.51; Michael Powers—p.55.